Eating Well on the Trail
A Guide to Homemade Hiking Meals

By
Trailname Ace

"A recipe has no soul. You as the cook must bring soul to the recipe."
    -Thomas Keller

This book is dedicated to my Little, who allows Daddy to pursue his passion of hiking as many trails, in as many places as possible.

Thank You

To Ahab and Bear Bait, who are two of the best hiking buddies that a guy could ask for.

To the many friends and family who have helped me by trying out my hiking meals, and who have encouraged me in the sport, and in the creation of this book.

To the Appalachian Trail, for kicking my butt on those sections, teaching me what I'm made of, and showing me how much tribulation that I'm able to overcome.

To Neon Sunrise Publishing for making it possible to publish this book.

And most importantly, to God, the Lord Almighty, for putting dreams in my heart, these people in my life, and for the strength to overcome and survive the hardships I've encountered on the trails.

"I can do all things through Christ who strengthens me."
Philippians 4:13

Table of Contents

The Backstory	4
Preparing a Meal on the Trail	11
A Happy Accident Ingredient	12
Nutritional Content of Meal Bulk	14

The Original Utility Meals — 15
Ace's Original Homemade Hiking Meal	17
Ace's Beefy Cheesy Potatoes	18
Ace's Original "On the Keto Side" Meal	19
Ace's Original Vegan Meal	20

Chicken
Ace's Chicken w/ Thai Peanut Sauce	23
Ace's Mom's Chicken Carbonara	24
Ace's Chicken Scampi	25
Ace's Chicken Curry	26
Ace's Chicken Mole	27
Ace's Chicken Alfredo	28
Ace's Brazilian Chicken w/Coconut Milk	29

Beef
Ace's Shepherd's Pie	30
Ace's Beef Stroganoff	31
Ace's Trail Tacos	32
Ace's All-American Goulash	33
Ace's Orange Beef	34
Ace's Beef & Broccoli	35

Soup and Stews
Ace's Chicken Tortilla Soup	37
Ace's Trail Chili	38
Ace's Shrimp Bisque	39
Ace's Chicken Noodle	40
Ace's Peanut Soup	41
Ace's Beef Stew	42
Ace's Stuffed Pepper Soup	43
Ace's Galumpki Soup	44
Ace's Chicken & Cabbage Curry Soup	45

Desserts
Ace's "Rice" Pudding	47
Ace's Chocolate Pudding	48
Ace's Hiker's Fuel Bars	49

The Backstory

When I first began getting into hiking, starting with planning a section hike on the Appalachian Trail, I was amazed at how much the hobby had evolved from my days hiking as a youth. Everything was lighter, stronger, more efficient in its use of space, and let's not forget... more expensive. Being a self-employed single father, my budget didn't allow for the purchase of the more through-hiker-friendly ultralight gear, so my research went in the direction of well-reviewed, cost-effective gear. Getting equipped was easy, but my hiking buddy, Ahab, and I kept running into the same issue; how to find nutritious, lightweight, space-saving, and cost-effective meals for our first five-day venture into the AT.

I began to think that it must be possible to prepare my own meals that would fit this bill. There are some commercially-available camp meals out there, that are pretty good... some can even be downright delicious. However, their cost, and/or the space they took up in the pack, kept driving me toward the goal of creating my own. One day as I was vacuum sealing my coffee beans in a mason jar, it dawned on me that I'd had the answer under my nose all along; the Foodsaver vacuum seal system. Not only would the machine be able to pack my meals down into the least possible space within the system's proprietary bags, but my meals would be sealed against rain, and wouldn't give off odor to attract unwelcome wildlife guests.

Making the Foodsaver bag system even more perfect for this purpose, is the fact that the bags are designed to be safely submerged within near-boiling water. This means that it's also safe to pour near-boiling water into the bag, to rehydrate any dehydrated and/or freeze-dried ingredients within the bag. The manufacturer has stated that the bags are also BPA-free, so there was no concern of those toxins leaching into my food. As an added benefit, since the Foodsaver bags were larger than I needed to transport and rehydrate my meals, I began to cut down the top of the bags, saving them to make smaller pouches to hold jerky, trail mix, Ace's Hiker's Fuel Bars, or other trail food... and even spare batteries, to keep them fresh and dry.

Having the solution as to how to pack the meals, I then set out to determine what to eat, based upon our nutritional needs of protein, carbs, and vitamins, primarily. After much searching, I landed on a sort of chili-mac noodle meal, consisting of ramen, freeze-dried ground beef, dehydrated vegetables, and instant chili mix. While those meals certainly did the job, and were a welcome sight at the end of a long day on the AT, they were basically just a utility meal. But they did what we needed them to do, they tasted good, and we knew what was in them.

About a year later, I started my YouTube channel, to help others get into hiking by sharing high-quality, low- (or lower-) cost hiking gear, in video reviews. One day, a friend told me that I needed to share my homemade hiking meal system, because the cost savings in using them over commercially-available meals was fairly substantial. I was surprised that I hadn't thought of it before, but it was a great idea, so I did my first hiking meal special.

Shortly after that video released, I had people ask me what to do if they're gluten intolerant. Being that I'm not a nutritionist, and have no training in it, I wanted to shy away from looking into the matter, but I saw it as a challenge, and an opportunity to share another homemade hiking meal video. Once I found the solution for replacing the ramen, I decided to look into another recipe, rather than just replacing the noodles.

Thinking I was done with recipes, I then received questions about how to create vegan hiking meals at home, which led me down another rabbit hole of research. Knowing that protein is probably the most elusive nutrient in vegan meals, I specifically searched for ingredients that would provide enough protein to properly sustain a vegan hiker. But this time, I also sought to bring a great flavor to the meal, and I wound up creating a meal that carried quite the umami. To date, this is my most costly homemade hiking meal, but it still came in at considerably less than the average camp meal that one can buy, and being that it fit a specialty diet, that's saying something.

In my search for the vegan meal's ingredients, I came across some ingredients that intrigued me, but didn't fit the bill for that meal; but I wanted to figure out how to use them. My next meal was my first that was more about flavor than sheer utility, though it still brought some good nutrition to the party. That meal was my Chicken with Thai Peanut Sauce. I was pretty proud of this one, and wanted a chef friend of mine to try it out and give me his opinions. He raved. As has everyone that has tried it. It's really that good. That recipe led me down the path to trying to create easy, light, cost-effective, packable meals, that will fully rehydrate with a little near-boiling water and a few minutes of time, all the while satisfying even the biggest foodies.

Again thinking that I was done with creating specialty-diet recipes, it caught me by surprise when Ahab told me that he'd gone Keto, and wondered what I could come up with for him. In researching what Keto hikers do for food, I was shocked to find that they were basically confined to living on jerky, nuts, and pepperoni. As a foodie, that was completely unacceptable to me. So I set out to find something to replace the noodles, while still providing bulk and flavor, and came up with a recipe that I found fairly enjoyable myself. But being that I don't like to ever just settle in once I find a solution, I kept looking. I eventually found a Keto-friendly dried pasta, that not only rehydrates quickly, but also brings additional nutrition over that contained within ramen.

With each recipe, I've included the approximate nutritional value of each meal, which may vary depending on the amounts of each ingredient you use, as well as the specific brand. Being that these are hiking meals, I've only included the "big seven" items; calories, fat, carbs, fiber, net carbs, protein, and sodium. Vitamin, calcium and other nutritional content have been left out to conserve space, and because they can vary greatly from brand to brand. Also, being that the nutritional values of the different "bulk" items such as noodles and their replacements greatly vary, I've included the approximate nutritional values of each, that can then be added to the values listed with each recipe, to make it easier for you to calculate the nutrition contained within your recipes upon modifying them.

Also, I recently became acutely aware of the sodium content in each of my meals and ingredients, as a result of helping to prepare hiking meals for a stroke survivor. You will most definitely want to pay close attention to the sodium content of your meals, and I would recommend that you consult with your medical professional prior to getting into the activity, and in the meal preparations for it.

You will also often see repetition of many of the same ingredients. I believe in being frugal and efficient with my money, so if I have to lay out money for a new ingredient, I want to make it as useful as possible within my hiking meal recipes. I encourage you to do the same, because in coming up with all of these recipes, I've accumulated quite a number of different ingredients, such that I have a dedicated section of my pantry strictly for hiking meal ingredients.

This book is here to help you start to create your own hiking meals, to save money, and feel better about knowing what you're eating. The beauty of the system, and the using of freeze-dried foods, is that you can manipulate the ingredients to suit your palate or your nutritional needs, without problem. You simply just need to possibly adjust the amount of water you add to the meal, to make sure that it's not too dry, nor too wet. I am including recipes for all of the meals that I mentioned above, as well as all of the others that I've created since. You can find links to the products I use, on my website: trailnameace.com. I hope you enjoy these recipes as much as I have enjoyed creating them, and yes, consuming them.

"A cookbook must have recipes, but it shouldn't be a blueprint. It should be more inspirational; it should be a guide."
-Thomas Keller

    It is my hope that this recipe book will inspire you to experiment with your own homemade hiking meals.

Preparing a Meal on the Trail

Preparing these meals couldn't be easier, nor more convenient. Rather than using a cooking system that I would then have to wash after eating (using precious water that you have to pack with you, and hope you have enough with you to last until the next water source), I simply slice the top of the bag open, and pour in near-boiling water. I find it best to add just enough to cover the ingredients, then let it sit while I set up my tent and get my gear stowed inside, or if I'm having lunch, to just sit and relax. You'll want to keep an eye on the water levels though, to ensure that one ingredient isn't soaking up all of the water and leaving other ingredients to be dry and/or chewy come meal time. This can take a little practice, but you'll quickly get the hang of it. The beauty of this is that you eat the meal right out of the bag, then put the bag in your ziplock trash bag, and cleanup is done. I can't think of a simpler, more convenient way to eat on the trail.

A Happy Accident Ingredient

While searching for ingredients for my vegan hiking meal, I kept coming up short on protein. That's when I found nutritional yeast. It was listed as a protein powerhouse, but little did I know the plethora of nutrients that it also carried. This one ingredient has so much nutrition, that I've begun adding varying amounts to almost all of my recipes; often adding 1Tbs. It has a slightly tangy flavor, that can hide itself pretty well in cheesy, spicy, or other meals that pack a lot of their own flavor.

In sweeter recipes, I usually forgo the nutritional yeast, but I think it best for you to experiment with your own palate, to determine how much or how little you would like to add. But even a little, will bring quite a bit of added nutrition through vitamins and other nutrients, that will only help to bolster you on those long trail days. This is what 1Tbs of the nutritional yeast that I use, brings to the table:

Potassium: 123mg Carbs: 5g   Fiber: 2g
Protein: 3g Vitamin B1: 273% Vitamin B2: 240%
Vitamin B3: 123% Vitamin B5:   5% Vitamin B6: 233%
Vitamin B12: 167% Folic Acid: 75% Biotin 100%

This vitamin content only scratches the surface. Nutritional yeast also contains a great number of minerals, amino acids, and other nutrients, in varying amounts, from trace to somewhat small. Also, considering that it has low net carbs, this ingredient can also add a nutritional boost to keto-friendly meals.

In creating my meal recipes, every meal I eat is the recipe that I'm working on, until I've reached the proportions that I find the most flavorful, while also meeting the nutritional requirements or limitations that I'm trying to meet. My suggestion for you, would be to make each meal in preparation, adding differing amounts of nutritional yeast until you find the amount that you find most palatable.

So, without further ado, let's get into the recipes!

Nutritional Content of Meal Bulk

Following is the content of the "bulk" of each meal, be it the ramen, the more keto-friendly noodles, potato shreds and so on. You will need to add these values to the nutritional values within each recipe, to allow you to determine the approximate nutritional value of the meal. If the ingredients list specifies a bulk item, then that nutritional information is included within the recipe's nutritional content. If the bulk isn't specified in the ingredients list, then I have left the nutritional information of the bulk out of those calculations, so that you can customize the recipes as you need to, and have an easier time of figuring out the nutritional content of the meal that you are preparing.

Ramen - 1 Block (Without Seasoning Packet)
Calories: 380 Carbs: 52g Fiber: 2g
Net Carbs: 50g
Fat: 14g Protein: 10g Sodium: 220mg
Iron: 20%

Dried Potato Shreds - 1 Cup
Calories: 220 Carbs: 48g Fiber: 4g
Net Carbs: 44g Fat: 0g Protein: 4g
Sodium: 900mg Iron: 4% Vitamin C: 40%
Calcium: 4%

Carba-Nada Noodles - 28g (3/4 Cup)
Calories: 85 Carbs: 12g Fiber: 4g
Net Carbs: 8g Fat: <1g Protein: 8g
Sodium: 8mg Iron: 5%
Calcium: 2%

Dried Riced Cauliflower - 16g

Calories:	9	Carbs:	2g	Fiber:	1g
Net Carbs:	1g	Fat:	0g	Protein:	1g
Sodium:	5mg	Iron:	1%	Vitamin C:	25%
Calcium:	1%				

Fonio - 1/4 Cup

Calories:	170	Carbs:	39g	Fiber:	1g
Net Carbs:	38g	Fat:	0.5g	Protein:	2g
Iron:	4%				

The Original Utility Meals

These first recipes were the result of needing to meet specific nutritional and/or dietary restrictions or requirements. My original meal was far more about nutrient and energy content, than it was about flavor, but as the other "specialty diet" recipes came along, I tried to bring more flavor to the meals as well.

When I came up with the recipe for the gluten-free option, I realized that I really liked the flavor, so I myself generally always carry one on my sections. That led me to try to bring great flavor to the subsequent meals, with the vegan option closely following the gluten-free option, when I had requests for assistance in finding vegan options; that meal presented quite the challenge, but I did come up with a recipe that offered a great umami flavor.

What follows are the original recipes that I came up with, which became the root of my experimenting in the kitchen to come up with even more.

Ace's Original Homemade Hiking Meal

This is the meal that I packed on my first days-long section on the AT. It's about the most basic meal you can get, and was designed specifically to be a utility meal. It did the job, and tasted great after a long day on the Trail, and it was perfect because it was inexpensive, light, and it didn't take much space.

Ingredients
1 Packet of Ramen, Crushed
20g Freeze-dried Ground Beef
1/4 Cup Freeze-dried Mixed Vegetables
3Tbs Instant Chili Mix

Nutritional Content
Calories: 649
Fat: 22g
Carbs: 83g
Fiber: 11g
Net Carbs: 72g
Protein: 45g
Sodium: 829mg

Ace's Beefy Cheesy Potatoes
(Original Gluten-Free Meal)

This recipe is the result of my search for a gluten-free option for a homemade hiking meal. I've found it to be quite enjoyable, but in looking into the sodium content, you may want to reduce the cheese powder to 2Tbs, instead of the 1/4 cup that I originally used. It's not as cheesy that way, but you also cut 450mg of sodium. If sodium isn't a big concern for you, then have at it! But I have found that any more than 1/4 cup makes the meal taste extremely salty.

Ingredients
1 Cup Dried Shredded Potatoes
30g Freeze-dried Ground Beef
1/4 Cup Cheese Powder (4 Tbs)

Nutritional Content		(With 2Tbs Cheese Instead)
Calories:	318	248
Fat:	20g	18g
Carbs:	48g	48g
Fiber:	0g	0g
Net Carbs:	48g	48g
Protein:	24g	20g
Sodium:	1281mg	831mg

Ace's Original "On the Keto Side" Meal

When Ahab told me that he'd gone Keto, and that he was planning on just eating jerky, pepperoni, and nuts on the trail, I found this to be completely unacceptable. So I set out to create meals that he could enjoy, while still keeping his net carbs low, and bringing flavor and fat to the meal. This is the original meal, that I've actually enjoyed myself!

Ingredients
16g Dried Riced Cauliflower
20g Freeze-dried Chicken
2Tbs Powdered Avocado
1Tbs Powdered Butter
1/4tsp Soy Sauce Powder

Nutritional Content
Calories:	320
Fat:	17g
Carbs:	13g
Fiber:	4g
Net Carbs:	9g
Protein:	19g
Sodium:	458mg

Ace's Original Vegan Meal

About the time that I started having people ask me about creating a vegan meal, my buddy, Bear Bait, decided that he wanted to start hiking, and he needed vegan meals. This allowed me to test out the recipe on a vegan, rather than just looking into what I found to have an appealing flavor. Since this meal, I've begun looking at ways to make my more foodie-friendly recipes to have a vegan option as well, because everyone should eat well on the trail!

Ingredients
1 Cup Fonio
35g Dried Tofu
2 tsp Spirulina Powder
28g Chopped Sun Dried Tomatoes
1 Sheet Nori
3 Tbs Nutritional Yeast

Nutritional Content
Calories: 200
Fat: 4g
Carbs: 33g
Fiber: 9g
Net Carbs: 24g
Protein: 20g
Sodium: 626mg

The Foodie-Friendly Meals

In my search to find ingredients for the specialty-diet meals, I kept coming across dried ingredients that didn't quite fit what I was looking for at that time, but intrigued me, and I wondered what I could create with them. The first recipe that I developed using these cool new ingredients, was the Chicken With Thai Peanut Sauce. Once I perfected the recipe, I had a few friends try it, one of them being a chef, and everyone raved over it. That inspired me to really get on the ball, to create as many foodie-friendly recipes as possible.

    The problem with creating these "gourmet" hiking meals, isn't in figuring out what to make. Nor is it in finding ingredients for them. The real challenge comes in finding not only dehydrated or freeze-dried ingredients, but also ones that rehydrate well, to make for a pleasing mouth feel, and to bring a good flavor to the meal. Many ingredients don't rehydrate well, leaving you to feel a little unsatisfied with the meal... anyone that has ever eaten a commercially-prepared, microwavable (or "add boiling water") cup of noodles meal, will know that the vegetables never properly rehydrate, remaining hard and crunchy, and bringing little, if any, flavor to the meal.

Sometimes, this can't be completely avoided, but I do my best to find good options for these dried ingredients, because my primary purpose in creating these meals is to have food for myself and my hiking buddies to eat on the trails. Some of my recipes still call for a vegetable soup mix, but I am also starting to move away from those, opting instead to add selections of specific vegetables into my meals. I do this to better calculate the nutritional values, as well as to have better control of the flavor and texture of the meal.

I can't stress this enough, but these recipes are just jumping-off points for you to start creating your own meals, and modify them to suit your own palate and/or dietary needs or restrictions. I hope you enjoy these following recipes as much as I do!

Ace's Chicken With Thai Peanut Sauce

As you've probably guessed by now, I'm quite proud of this one. This recipe has become my favorite hiking meal to pack, and the smell once it's prepared in the camp site, has made more than a few other hikers jealous. This meal can easily become Keto-friendly, and vegan, so there's no excuse not to eat an amazing meal on the trail! I usually do this one with ramen, for mouth feel and authenticity.

Ingredients
20g Freeze-Dried Chicken
1Tbs Freeze-Dried Mixed Vegetables
2Tbs Peanut Butter Powder
1Tbs Coconut Milk Powder
1/2Tsp Soy Sauce Powder
1/2Tsp Powdered Lime

Nutritional Content
Calories: 226
Fat: 10g
Carbs: 11g
Fiber: 4g
Net Carbs: 7g
Protein: 24g
Sodium: 574mg

Ace's Mom's Chicken Carbonara

When I found the freeze-dried peas, I just had to find a recipe for them. Then I remembered that my mom used to make a chicken carbonara that we would rave over. So, I started looking into carbonara recipes... that's when I realized that my mom had married carbonara with alfredo. In honor of my mom, I created this recipe to replicate that which she made fresh, and which we loved. It's not a traditional carbonara, but it reminds me of how creative my mom was in the kitchen. I usually use ramen with this meal, too.

Ingredients
20g Chicken
14g (1 Strip) Bacon Jerky (chopped)
7g Freeze-dried Peas
1/2Tsp Garlic Powder
1/2Tsp Italian Seasoning
3Tbs Powdered Milk
2Tbs Powdered Butter
6 Packets (2Tbs) Parmesan Cheese
(seal packets in pouch)

Nutritional Content
Calories: 573
Carbs: 25g
Sodium: 276mg
Fat: 37g
Fiber: 2g
Protein: 36g
Net Carbs: 23g

Ace's Chicken Scampi

As I was making a Shrimp Scampi dinner for my Little one evening, I realized that I had most of the ingredients in my hiking pantry, to try to create one for a hiking meal. When I added the white wine at the end, I realized that a Scampi may be difficult at best, because how easy could it be to find a powdered white wine? Well, your buddy Ace pulled it off, and found a white wine powder. You could make a Scampi without the wine, but it would be greatly lacking in the flavor department. This is now one of my main go-to meals, that I include on every section! I usually use the Carba-Nada noodles with this (Lemon Pepper).

Ingredients
20g Freeze-dried Chicken
1/4 tsp Lemon Powder
2 Tbs Powdered Butter
1/2 tsp Italian Seasoning
5 Pieces Freeze-dried Sliced Garlic
1/4 tsp Garlic Powder
1 tsp White Wine Powder

Nutritional Content
Calories: 190
Net Carbs: 1g
Sodium: 381mg
Carbs: 1g
Fat: 12g
Fiber: 0g
Protein: 24g

Ace's Chicken Curry

I'm a huge fan of Indian food, and thought that a nice curry would be amazing after a long day on the trail. Once I discovered tomato powder, I knew that this could easily be achieved. To date, I haven't found a rice product that would hold up for long, or that would hydrate well, so I called upon my friend, the dried riced cauliflower to fill the bulk of this meal. This curry is not only satisfying, but the aroma of the spices makes for an incredible dining experience on the trail!

Ingredients
16g Dried Riced Cauliflower
20g Freeze-dried Chicken
1/2 tsp Freeze-dried Onion
7g Freeze-dried Peas
1 Packet Sodium-free Chicken Stock Powder
1 1/2 tsp Tomato Powder
2 Tbs Coconut Milk Powder
1 Tbs Powdered Butter
1/4 tsp Garlic Powder
3/4 tsp Curry Powder

Nutritional Content
Calories:	379
Net Carbs:	14g
Sodium:	311mg
Carbs:	22g
Fat:	21g
Fiber:	8g
Protein:	26g

Ace's Chicken Mole

I love this traditional Mexican dish normally, so when I was making it for dinner one night, it just hit me that I needed to make a hiking meal version of it. There's a lot going on with this dish, and it hits your tastebuds with all sorts of sensations. I always make it with cayenne pepper for the heat, but it also adds something to the flavor profile that is noticeably missing if it's not added. I start with 1/4 teaspoon in my own meals, but I've cut that in half for this recipe, in case you're not a pepper head.

Ingredients
20g Chicken
8g Riced Cauliflower
1 tsp Onion Flakes
1/2 tsp Garlic Powder
1/2 tsp Chili Powder
1/8 tsp Cinnamon
1/8 tsp Cumin
1/4 tsp Oregano
1 tsp Chicken Broth
1 tsp Peanut Butter Powder
1 tsp Tomato Powder
1 tsp Cacao
1 Tbs Butter Powder
1/8 tsp Cayenne Pepper

Nutritional Content
Calories: 275
Sodium: 388mg
Fat: 15g
Carbs: 14g
Fiber: 5g
Net Carbs: 9g
Protein: 25g

Ace's Chicken Alfredo

This one has tasted like restaurant quality Alfredo every time I've had it. The sauce tends to be considerably thinner than what you'll have in a restaurant or at home, but the flavor is there! I usually make this one with the Carba-Nada egg noodles, for that al dente pasta texture.

Ingredients
20g Chicken
1 Tbs Butter Powder
2 Tbs Heavy Cream Powder
1 Tbs Parmesan (3 Packets)
(seal packets in pouch)
1 Tbs Cream Cheese Powder
1 tsp Chicken Broth Powder
1/4 tsp Italian Seasoning
6 Pieces Sliced Garlic
1/2 tsp Garlic Powder
1/2 tsp White Wine Powder
Pinch Black Pepper

Nutritional Content
Calories: 314
Net Carbs: 3g
Fat: 23g
Protein: 23g
Carbs: 3g
Sodium: 687mg
Fiber: 0g

Ace's Brazilian Chicken with Coconut Milk

This dish is another in my search to make the most use, and in the largest variety of ways, of each of the ingredients that I purchase for my homemade hiking meal pantry. It is another where you will want to experiment with the level of heat that you want to add to the recipe, but I've found that eliminating the cayenne shallows the depth of flavor of this dish. I usually make this with the cauliflower, but it goes well with ramen, too.

Ingredients
20g Chicken
1 Tbs Coconut Milk
1 tsp Onion Flakes
1 tsp Chicken Bone Broth
1/2 tsp Tomato Powder
1/4 tsp Cumin
6 Pieces Sliced Garlic
1/4 tsp Turmeric
1/4 tsp Coriander
1/2 tsp Ginger
1/2 tsp Garlic Powder
1/4 tsp Cayenne Pepper
Pinch Red Pepper Flake
Pinch Italian Seasoning

Nutritional Content
Calories: 159
Fat: 8g
Carbs: 7g
Fiber: 3g
Net Carbs: 4g
Protein: 22g
Sodium: 338mg

Ace's Shepherd's Pie

One of my favorite comfort foods is shepherd's pie. What's not to love about mashed potatoes, beef, and peas and carrots, all served up together? This meal can easily be made Keto, by replacing the potatoes with the dried riced cauliflower. If you do so, just subtract from these nutritional values, 90 calories, 20g carbs, 2g fiber (18g net carbs), 2g protein, and 180mg of sodium, and add the values from the dried riced cauliflower. Though you'll want to play with these ingredients to see if the change in flavor and texture is worth a few carbs.

Ingredients
25g Instant Mashed Potatoes
1Tbs Powdered Butter
7g Freeze-dried Peas
7g (~1Tbs) Freeze-dried carrots
20g Freeze-dried Ground Beef

Nutritional Content
Calories: 361
Carbs: 34g
Fiber: 5g
Net Carbs: 29g
Fat: 18g
Protein: 18g
Sodium: 562mg

Ace's Beef Stroganoff

In keeping with the comfort food theme, who doesn't love Beef Stroganoff? It has always been one of my favorite dishes. I wanted to experiment with freeze-dried mushrooms, and this was the first recipe that popped into my head. The hard part for this recipe, was finding a powdered beef stock, especially one that was low sodium. Being that I wasn't having much luck, I discovered a low sodium beef gravy mix, and love it. It tastes so much better than just "brown." I use the Carba-Nada egg noodles with this one.

Ingredients
20g Freeze-dried Ground Beef
2Tbs Powdered Sour Cream
1Tbs Powdered Butter
2g Freeze-dried Mushrooms
1Tsp Freeze-dried Onions
1Tbs Low Sodium Beef Gravy Mix
1/4Tsp Garlic Powder

Nutritional Content
Calories: 386
Protein: 20g
Carb: 19g
Fiber: 1g
Net Carbs: 18g
Fat: 35g
Sodium: 604mg

Ace's Trail Tacos

One thing that I've noticed many people longing for on the trails, are tacos and burritos. I have found a way to bring these to the trail, adding a little variety to the trip, not having to eat from a bag every meal. I start by rolling tortillas up in parchment paper, then vacuum sealing them in a cut-down Foodsaver bag. This saves space, and helps to protect the tortillas from damage in the pack. My Trail Taco filling tends to come out a little thicker-sauced and a bit more like a classic mole recipe than a taco recipe, but Ahab and I have both rather enjoyed them on the Trail. Check my website for keto-friendly tortilla options!

Ingredients
20g Beef
1/2 Tbs tomato powder
1 Tbs beef gravy mix
1 tsp diced onion
1/2 tsp garlic powder

1 Tbs chili powder
2 tsp paprika
1 tsp cumin
1 tsp coriander
1/2 tsp oregano

Nutritional Content
Calories: 147
Sodium: 419mg
Fat: 9g
Carbs: 22g
Fiber: 4g
Net Carbs: 18g
Protein: 15g

Ace's All-American Goulash

This one got its name because a Polish friend of mine informed me that Americans always make goulash wrong. While my palate tends toward as authentic a taste as possible, in this case I got my inspiration from the goulash that I grew up with. I usually always make this one with the Carba-Nada egg noodles because egg noodles are what I grew up with, but it would work just as well with ramen. If you want to cut the carbs a bit more, you could eliminate the beef gravy mix and replace it with beef or chicken broth powder, which would shave 5g of carbs. But I prefer the deeper flavor of the gravy mix, personally.

Ingredients
30g Beef
6 Pieces Sliced Garlic
1/8 tsp Soy Sauce Powder
1 tsp Paprika
1/2 tsp Garlic Powder
1/4 tsp Italian Seasoning
1 tsp Onion Flakes
1 Tbs Tomato Powder
1 Tbs Beef Gravy
2 Tbs Bell Pepper

Nutritional Content
Calories: 267
Sodium: 539mg
Fat: 15g
Carbs: 17g
Fiber: 5g
Net Carbs: 12g
Protein: 19g

Ace's Orange Beef

This is hands-down my favorite dish in Chinese restaurants. When I happened upon dried orange rind, I knew that I had to come up with an Orange Beef recipe. This can just as easily be made into Orange Chicken, but with the number of chicken recipes that I already had, I decided to go with my favorite. I included the riced cauliflower in this, but if you decide to eliminate that and replace the bulk with ramen (which I'd recommend if you're not keto), you'll probably be just that much happier! Just remove half of the listed nutritional content of the cauliflower from the beginning of the book.

Ingredients
30g Beef
8g Riced Cauliflower
2 tsp Orange Zest Powder
1/4 tsp Soy Sauce Powder
1 tsp Sherry Powder
1/2 tsp Garlic Powder
1/4 tsp Dried Orange Zest (Optional)

1 Tbs Butter Powder
1/2 tsp Ginger
1/2 Tbs Agave Inulin
1 tsp Honey Powder
Pinch Red Pepper
6 Pieces Sliced Garlic

Nutritional Content
Calories: 354
Carbs: 21g
Fiber: 9g
Net Carbs: 12g
Sodium: 382mg
Fat: 26g
Protein: 21g

Ace's Beef & Broccoli

Here's another classic favorite. When I discovered the freeze dried broccoli, I knew that I had to try to come up with a recipe for one of the most popular Chinese dishes this side of the Pacific. To keep it keto, I went with dried riced cauliflower, but you could easily replace it with ramen if you wanted more texture, and carbs aren't a big issue for you. If you stick with the cauliflower, you'll need to babysit the meal a bit more after you add the water, because the cauliflower gets pretty greedy for the water, soaking it up really quickly, so you'll need to add small amounts at a time until everything is hydrated properly.

Ingredients
20g Beef
16g Riced Cauliflower
1 tsp Onion Flakes
7g Broccoli
1/4 tsp Soy Sauce Powder
1 tsp Garlic Powder
1/2 tsp Ginger Powder
1 tsp Agave Inulin
Pinch Black Pepper
1/2 tsp Sherry Powder
6 Pieces Sliced Garlic
1 tsp Broth Powder
1/8 tsp Beef Gravy Mix
1/8 tsp Sesame Seeds

Nutritional Content
Calories: 180
Carbs: 23g
Fiber: 12g
Net Carbs: 11g
Fat: 10g
Protein: 22g
Sodium: 375mg

Soups & Stews

Few things are as enjoyable on a cold evening, as a nice, hot soup or stew. I generally plan my hiking trips around the cold weather, because it makes for a more comfortable hike, and even better sleeping conditions. On the colder nights, I love to break out one of these soup or stew pouches, sit back, relax, and listen to the sounds at the shelters, usually interspersed with the sound of other hikers grumbling about their meager meal options. One of the best parts of using my soup and stew recipes, is that the amount of water isn't nearly as crucial as it is when I'm just using it to rehydrate my ingredients and create a sauce. Soups are much more forgiving, and allow for a greater amount of water to be added, allowing me to focus more on setting up camp, than on continuing to monitor and add water to my meal pouch.

Ace's Chicken Tortilla Soup

This Mexican dish is as flexible as you want it to be. The base recipe is pleasant and bright thanks to the lime, and can be done "naked" or with a little more heat to kick it up.

<u>Ingredients</u>
20g Chicken
1 tsp diced onion
6 pieces of dried garlic
1 tsp tomato powder
7g black beans
8g chili lime tortilla chips
1/2 tsp garlic powder
1 tsp chicken broth powder
1 tsp lime powder
1/2 tsp red pepper flakes

<u>Nutritional Content</u>
Calories:	189
Fat:	6g
Carbs:	12g
Fiber:	4g
Net Carbs:	8g
Protein:	23g
Sodium:	356mg

Ace's Trail Chili

Few things are as welcome and enjoyable next to a campfire, more than a good, hearty chili. I like this one so much, that on cold nights at home, I'll often make it and go sit by my fire in the back yard!

Ingredients
30g Beef
7g Kidney Beans
1 Tbs Tomato Powder
1 Tbs Avocado Powder
6 Pieces Sliced Garlic
1 tsp Onion Flakes
1 tsp Chicken Bone Broth
1/4 tsp Lime Powder
1 tsp Chili Powder
1/8 tsp Paprika
1/2 tsp Garlic Powder
9g Freeze Dried Cheese

Nutritional Content
Calories: 342
Protein: 27g
Fat: 21g
Carbs: 14g
Fiber: 5g
Net Carbs: 9g
Sodium: 540mg

Ace's Shrimp Bisque

Ok, if you've caught any of my recipe videos on my YouTube channel, you'll have come to the realization that I'm a diehard foodie. You can be just as rustic, exotic, or gastronomic as you'd like to be on the trails, and this recipe proves it. This is another one that I've been known to make at home, because it's quick and tasty!

Ingredients
3 Tbs Shrimp Powder
3 Tbs Heavy Cream Powder
1 Tbs Cream Cheese Powder
1/2 Tbs Butter Powder
4 Pieces Sliced Garlic
1 tsp Onion Flakes
1/2 Tbs Tomato Powder
1 tsp Sherry Powder
1/2 tsp Garlic Powder

Nutritional Content
Calories: 226
Fat: 18g
Carbs: 9g
Fiber: 2g
Net Carbs: 7g
Protein: 8g
Sodium: 283mg

Ace's Chicken Noodle

Let's face it, no good trail food recipe book would be complete without one of the world's most popular comfort foods. This one carries all of the flavor, comfort, and nutrition of its homemade counterpart, with the convenience of being able to pack it out.

Ingredients
20g Chicken
4g Celery
5 Pieces Sliced Garlic
1 tsp Onion Flakes
1 Tbs Carrot
1 Tbs Chicken Bone Broth
1/2 tsp Garlic Powder
1/4 tsp Italian Seasoning
1 tsp Avocado Powder
1 tsp White Wine Powder
Noodles of Your Choice (Not Included in Nutritional Content)

Nutritional Content
Calories: 173
Fat: 5g
Carbs: 13g
Fiber: 5g
Net Carbs: 8g
Protein: 21g
Sodium: 435mg

Ace's Peanut Soup

Being that I try to find the most uses out of each ingredient in my trail meal pantry, I began to look for new uses for the peanut butter powder that I used in my Chicken with Thai Peanut Sauce recipe. I came across a West African peanut soup that sounded great to me. While this recipe varies from the original recipe that I found, I believe that my iteration pays homage to the recipe that inspired it.

Ingredients
20g Chicken
2 Tbs Peanut Butter Powder
1 tsp Chicken Bone Broth
2 Tbs Cream Cheese Powder
1 tsp Avocado Powder
1 tsp Onion Flakes
1/2 tsp Garlic Powder
1/4 tsp Italian Seasoning

1/2 tsp Ginger
8 Pieces Sliced Garlic
1/2 Tbs Carrot
4g Broccoli
1/4 tsp Celery
1/8 tsp Red Pepper

Nutritional Content
Calories: 294
Fat: 15g
Carbs: 16g
Fiber: 7g
Net Carbs: 9g
Protein: 27g
Sodium: 516mg

Ace's Beef Stew

Here's another big hit on the Trails. It's hearty, tasty, and feels like being at home while enjoying the freedom of the wilderness. I'd be remiss if I didn't include a beef stew recipe, being that dried ground beef is one of my most-used ingredients. This is another one that has people in shelters jealous of my meal choices! If you want to go extra-keto, you could eliminate the potato shreds, but they only add 3g Net Carbs, while adding a great tooth to the meal.

Ingredients
30g Beef
5g Potato Shreds
1 tsp Onion Flakes
1 tsp Carrot
1/4 tsp Celery
1 tsp Beef Gravy Mix
6 Pieces Sliced Garlic
1/2 tsp Garlic Powder
1/4 tsp Paprika
1 tsp Sherry Powder
1 tsp Avocado Powder
1/4 tsp Italian Seasoning
1 tsp Chicken Bone Broth
1 Tbs Cream Cheese Powder

Nutritional Content
Calories: 328
Fat: 23g
Carbs: 17g
Fiber: 5g
Net Carbs: 12g
Protein: 23g
Sodium: 754mg

Ace's Stuffed Pepper Soup

Inspiration for dishes can come from the most unusual places, and this one came to me in the form of a popup ad online. All I had to see was the name of the dish, and I knew that I needed to create my own version of it. I set out by thinking about what I put in a stuffed bell pepper, and the recipe just flowed from there. This soup is really hearty, very tasty, and quite keto.

Ingredients
20g Beef
7g Bell Pepper (About 3 Tbs)
1 tsp Onion Flakes
4g Riced Cauliflower
4g Tomato Flakes
6 Pieces Sliced Garlic
1 tsp Tomato Powder
1/8 tsp Beef Gravy Mix
1/4 tsp Italian Seasoning
1/2 tsp Garlic Powder
1 tsp Chicken Broth
1 Tbs Butter

Nutritional Content
Calories: 247
Fat: 11g
Carbs: 18g
Fiber: 6g
Net Carbs: 12g
Protein: 21g
Sodium: 363mg

Ace's Galumpki Soup

This is another dish that was inspired by a new ingredient that intrigued me and made me want to come up with a recipe for it; this one was freeze dried cabbage. Not wanting to just do another cabbage soup, I took inspiration from the Polish dish galumpki, which is stuffed cabbage leaves. I think it translated very well into a soup, with all of the essential flavors in there. The cabbage keeps a nice, crunchy texture, making for a pleasant dining experience!

Ingredients
20g Beef
9g Cabbage (~2 1/2" Tbs)
1 Tbs Tomato Flakes
1 tsp Onion Flakes
1 tsp Tomato Powder
4g Riced Cauliflower
1 Tbs Butter Powder
6 Pieces Sliced Garlic
1 Tbs Red Wine Powder
1/4 tsp Italian Seasoning
1/2 tsp Garlic Powder
1 tsp Chicken Broth
1/4 tsp Paprika

Nutritional Content
Calories: 264
Fat: 20g
Carbs: 19g
Fiber: 5g
Net Carbs: 14g
Protein: 20g
Sodium: 347mg

Ace's Chicken & Cabbage Curry Soup

Having the cabbage in my pantry caused me to start looking around at other ways to use it. Sitting in an Indian restaurant one day, I saw chicken and cabbage curry on the menu, and the inspiration hit me. Rather than another curry dish with riced cauliflower, I decided to start looking into creating a soup with the inspiration that that Indian dish provided. I hope you enjoy it!

Ingredients
20g Chicken
9g Cabbage (~2 1/2 Tbs)
1 tsp Onion Flakes
6 Pieces Sliced Garlic
1 tsp Chicken Broth
1 Tbs Coconut Milk Powder
1/2 tsp Curry Powder
1/2 tsp Garlic Powder
1 Tbs Butter Powder
1 tsp Peanut Butter Powder
Pinch Black Pepper

Nutritional Content
Calories: 296
Fat: 19g
Carbs: 13g
Fiber: 2g
Net Carbs: 11g
Protein: 22g
Sodium: 343mg

Desserts

I've included this section as a separate section, even though my desserts are, to date, actually meals disguising themselves as desserts. On my AT sections, the biggest complaints I hear from other hikers, is that they miss their candy bars. Now, there are some great products out there for desserts, such as the ice cream sandwiches and cheesecake bites by Mountain House, which are both amazing, but they do have their down sides; they are more fragile, so you're fairly likely to leave crumbs around your campsite, which will increase your chances of unwelcome wildlife guests; and they tend to be a bit pricey.

One day while I was organizing my pantry, I came across an ingredient that I thought could easily be used to bring a nice dessert on the Trail, that was cost-effective, lightweight, durable (since it would be vacuum sealed like my other meals), tasty, and nutritious. Following are the two recipes that I came up with, that pack a pretty good wallop in the nutrition department, all the while making you feel like you're being bad on the trail.

Ace's "Rice" Pudding

This was my first "dessert" that I began to play with, and once I nailed down the proportions, I looked into the nutritional content. I was amazed at the protein and fat content, both of which are the Keto hiker's best friends. If you want to do this recipe as a Keto meal though, you'll probably want to eliminate the raisins, because they add 15 net carbs by themselves. This pudding does have a bit of a crunch to it, due to the seeds, but I personally don't find that off-putting. I hope you enjoy my stealth dessert!

Ingredients
1/4 Cup Chia Seeds
3Tbs Whole Milk Powder
1Tsp Powdered Butter
1/2Tbs Vanilla Sugar
2Tbs Raisins

Nutritional Content
Calories: 469
Carb: 51g
Fiber: 21g
Net Carbs: 30g
Protein: 19g
Fat: 21g
Calcium: 52%
Iron: 20%
Omega-3:   12g
Magnesium: 40%

Ace's Chocolate Pudding

One evening while whipping up a batch of my homemade hot cocoa to settle in with the Little to watch Polar Express, it dawned on me that I could create a chocolate pudding to take on the trail with me, simply by modifying my "Rice" Pudding recipe. I like a stronger, darker chocolate flavor in my chocolate treats, so you may want to cut the amount of cacao in half to start, but I've found this dessert to be a real treat on the trail!

Ingredients
1/4 Cup Chia Seeds
3Tbs Whole Milk Powder
2Tbs Raw Cacao Powder
1/2Tbs Vanilla Sugar

Nutritional Content
Calories: 424
Carb: 41g
Fiber: 20g
Net Carbs: 21g
Protein: 20g
Fat: 21g
Calcium: 50%
Iron: 17%
Magnesium: 48%
Omega-3:   12g

Ace's Hiker's Fuel Bars

When Ahab and I started planning our first section on the AT, this was another item that I knew I had to create, to cut the costs of having to buy commercially-made energy bars at the $2-5 cost per bar. Having some skills in the kitchen, I started looking at what we thought our needs would be for a quick, yet sustaining source of energy for our breakfast. The first iteration was ok, and provided energy for the mornings where I was training for my first trek, but the bars left a lot to be desired where flavor was concerned. I sat down with my notes and started brainstorming. After a couple of minor tweaks (the second and third batches were well received, but I continued to play with the recipe to try to optimize the flavor profiles, and maximize the energy and nutritional value that the bars would provide), I finally nailed down exactly what I wanted to use on the Trail.

For my first section on the AT, I cut this recipe into eight relatively evenly-sized bars, but they proved to weigh a little heavily on the gut within an hour, so I've since reduced their size to sixteen bars; the half-sized bars do the job well, don't get heavy on the stomach, and fit nicely in a pocket for those moments where you need a boost but aren't ready or able to sit down and enjoy one of my homemade hiking meals. I have included the approximate "big seven" nutritional content of the entire batch, as well as that of the bar that is roughly 1/16 of the total. For the record, these aren't even remotely keto!

Ingredients
- 1/2 Cup Vanilla Almond Butter
- 1/2 Cup Chocolate Hazelnut Butter
- 1/2 Cup Honey
- 3 Cups Rolled Oats
- 2/3 Cup Hemp Hearts (Ground Into a Powder)
- 1/4 Cup Nutritional Yeast
- 1 Cup Dates (Pitted and Thoroughly Chopped)

The Process
In a large pot, heat the almond butter, hazelnut butter, and honey over medium heat, stirring frequently until thoroughly blended. Once the mixture has softened well and the individual ingredients are no longer distinguishable from each other, add the ground hemp hearts and nutritional yeast, stirring well to evenly distribute the ingredients in the honey-nut butter mixture. Upon achieving a good, even paste, add the oats and chopped dates, stirring and folding constantly to evenly coat all of the oats and distribute the dates throughout. This one can take some time, but it comes together soon enough.

While still hot, spoon the mixture into a parchment-lined 9x7 baking dish, evenly smoothing it to a consistent thickness, packing it down well. At this point, score the top of the mixture with a knife, to mark where you plan to cut your bars down to size. After this, place the baking dish into the freezer for 30 to 45 minutes, just long enough for the bars to solidify enough to allow for cutting. Remove the bars on the parchment, moving the mass to a cutting board. Use a chef's knife to carefully cut the bars to size, cutting all the way through. Then transfer the bars back to the freezer to fully freeze overnight.

Once your bars are frozen solid, create pouches for your bars from the remnants of the cut-down Foodsaver bags that you have used to store your homemade hiking meals. Add one bar to a pouch just big enough to hold it and allow for Foodsaver operation, then vacuum seal the frozen bar in the pouch. The reason I freeze them is to prevent them from squashing down during the vacuum sealing process, and the square-cut bars just make it easier to pack and eat. Once they're all sealed, I pop them back in the freezer to store them for long term, or into my hiking food stash if I have a trip coming up soon.

It can be a bit time-consuming, but you won't regret putting in the effort for that flavor, and your wallet will thank you!

Approximate Nutritional Content

	Entire Batch	1 Bar (at ~ 1/16 Size)
Calories:	3985	249
Fat:	156g	10g
Carbs:	593g	37g
Fiber:	71g	4g
Net Carbs:	522g	33g
Protein:	107g	7g
Sodium:	797mg	50mg

Ace started his namesake YouTube channel, Trailname Ace, as a way to share his knowledge and experiences with finding quality, cost-effective hiking and camping gear.

At the suggestion of his friends, Ace released a video covering his homemade hiking meals, and how inexpensively they could be made. That led to multiple special-diet meals for the trails, and eventually getting into more gourmet, foodie friendly meals. Ace discovered that even his most expensive specialty-diet meals came in at far less than most commercially-available camp meals, so he made it a goal to develop as many meals as possible to increase variety and dining pleasure on the trails.

Ace continues to develop new meals all the time, as well as reviewing new hiking gear as he finds a need and/or has a request to review a product. His goal is to encourage people to engage in the sport, by showing them that it doesn't have to be an overly expensive activity.

Make sure to subscribe to his channel, and let him know that Neon Sunrise sent you!

Neon Sunrise Publishing is focused on helping independent creators realize their dreams of seeing their books in print. We're driven by a DIY spirit and a desire to provide options and resources to help developing talent succeed in sharing their voice with the world.

To keep up with all of our latest news and releases, be sure to join our mailing list and connect with us online!

Email: neonsunrisepub@gmail.com
Facebook: facebook.com/neonsunrisepub
Instagram: @neonsunrisepub
Twitter: @neonsunrisepub
Website: www.neonsunrisepublishing.com

© 2020 Trailname Ace
A Neon Sunrise Publication. All Rights Reserved

www.ingramcontent.com/pod-product-compliance
Lightning Source LLC
Chambersburg PA
CBHW031504040426
42444CB00007B/1203